G5 > M2 > WIT & WISDOM™

GREAT MINDS® WIT & WISDOM

Grade 5 Module 2:
Word Play

Student Edition

Copyright © 2016 Great Minds®

COPYRIGHT STATEMENT

Published by Great Minds®.

Copyright ©2016 Great Minds®. All rights reserved. No part of this work may be reproduced or used in any form or by any means—graphic, electronic, or mechanical, including photocopying or information storage and retrieval systems—without written permission from the copyright holder.

ISBN: 978-1-68386-038-9

Table of Contents

GRADE 5 MODULE 2

Handout 1A: Assessed Vocabulary Study Guide

Handout 2A: Fluency Homework

Handout 2B: Frayer Model

Handout 3A: "Who's on First?"

Handout 4A: Speaking and Listening Style Checklist

Handout 5A: Fluency Homework

Handout 6A: Setting and Character Analysis Chart

Handout 6B: Precise Words

Handout 7A: Story Map

Handout 8A: Observe-Infer-Wonder Chart

Handout 8B: Fluency Homework

Handout 8C: Precise Words

Handout 9A: Painting Analysis Chart

Handout 9B: Setting Snapshot

Handout 10A: "Tired" Words and Some Punchier Alternatives

Handout 11A: Character Snapshot

Handout 12A: Frayer Model

Handout 12B: Character Snapshot Planner

Handout 13A: Oral Story Map

Handout 13B: Fluency Homework

Handout 14A: Think-Pair-Square-Share with Adages

Handout 15A: Focusing Question Task 2 Checklist

Handout 16A: Plot Flowcharts

Handout 16B: Fluency Homework

Handout 16C: Synonym Quest

Handout 17A: ESCAPE Structure for Narrative Stories

Handout 18A: Exploded Moment Model

Handout 19A: Milo's Gifts

Handout 19B: Exploded Moment Planner

Handout 19C: Fluency Homework

Handout 20A: Dialogue Quest

Handout 21A: Story Map

Handout 22A: Dialogue Planner

Handout 22B: Conventions of Dialogue-Writing

Handout 25A: Focusing Question Task 3 Checklist

Handout 26A: Fluency Homework

Handout 27A: Demons of Ignorance

Handout 28A: Demons of Ignorance Homework

Handout 29A: Rhyme and Reason's Advice

Handout 29B: Fluency Homework

Handout 32A: Theme Paragraph Planner

Handout 33A: *Reading at a Table*

Handout 33B: Museum Label for Magritte

Handout 33C: Museum Label for Dali

Handout 33D: Focusing Question Task 4 Checklist

Handout 34A: Demon Analysis

Handout 35A: Dialogue Planner for End-of-Module Task

Handout 36A: End-of-Module Task Checklist

Volume of Reading Reflection Questions

Wit & Wisdom Parent Tip Sheet

Handout 1A: Assessed Vocabulary Study Guide

Directions: Use this list of vocabulary words and definitions to study for the vocabulary assessment. The number following the word indicates the lesson number in which the word or affix is taught.

Word (Lesson Number)	Definition
wordplay (1)	Playful or clever use of words to create humor.
peculiar (2)	Abnormal or different from the usual expectation.
wisdom (5)	Accumulated knowledge or learning.
ignorance (5, 27)	A state of not knowing; lack of awareness or education.
expectations (6)	Beliefs or hopes concerning what is possible in the future.
doldrums (6)	A boring, gloomy place, or state of mind, in which nothing happens.
lethargy (6)	A state of having very low energy with drowsiness and lack of interest or feeling; sloth, indifference, idleness, inactivity.
killing time (7)	Wasting time.
diction (8)	Choice of words in speech or writing.
surreal (9, 33)	Bizarre, weird, or eerie; having a dream-like quality; beyond real, very strange or unusual.
humbug (10)	A person involved in an act meant to trick or deceive someone; someone who pretends to be someone he is not; a dishonest or insincere person; nonsense; faker, fraud, impostor, phony.
macabre (12)	Of, dealing with, or pertianing to death or the horrors of death; gruesome.
corrupts (12)	To cause to become harmed or damaged.
rhyme or reason (13)	Having or showing good sense, logic, or meaning.
disputes (13)	Arguments or debates; things that people do not agree on.

Name: _____

Date: _____

eat my words (14)	To admit that what you said is wrong.
make hay while the sun shines (14)	To take advantage of an opportunity or get something done while you have the chance.
leave no stone unturned (14)	To consider every possibility when trying to solve a problem.
quest (20)	A journey made in search of something; expedition; adventure.
point of view (17)	1. A place from which you see something. 2. The way in which one thinks about a situation or event.
discord (20)	A combination of sounds that is unpleasant.
din (20)	A loud ongoing noise; racket; clamor.
disconsolate (prefix) (21)	Not or lack of (definition of *dis-*).
jump to conclusions (23)	To decide something quickly without having a good reason for it.
transformation (27)	A major change in someone or something.
trivial (27)	Of little value or importance; petty, small.
insincerity (28)	The act of being phony or fake.
gelatinous (28)	Like jelly or gelatin, especially in consistency.
conspicu**ous** (suffix) (28)	Having much or full of; characterized by (definition of *-ous*).
castles in the air (29)	Dreams, plans, and/or hopes that are unrealistic, impossible, or otherwise have very little chance of happening.

Handout 2A: Fluency Homework

Directions:
1. Day 1: Read the text carefully and annotate to help you read fluently.
2. Each day:
    a. Practice reading the text three to five times.
    b. Evaluate your progress by placing a ✓+, ✓, or ✓- in each unshaded box.
    c. Ask someone (adult or peer) to listen and evaluate you as well.
3. Last day: Respond to the self-reflection questions.

Abbott: Well Costello, I'm going to New York with you. You know Bucky Harris, the Yankees' manager, gave me a job as coach for as long as you're on the team.

Costello: Look Abbott, if you're the coach, you must know all the players.

Abbott: I certainly do.

Costello: Well you know I've never met the guys. So you'll have to tell me their names, and then I'll know who's playing on the team.

Abbott: Oh, I'll tell you their names, but you know it seems to me they give these ball players now-a-days very peculiar names.

Costello: You mean funny names?

Abbott: Strange names, pet names...Well, let's see, we have on the bags, Who's on first, What's on second, I Don't Know is on third...

Costello: That's what I want to find out.

Abbott: I say Who's on first, What's on second, I Don't Know's on third.

Abbott, William, and Lou Costello. "Who's on First?" Baseball Almanac. Web. 8 June 2016. <http://www.baseball-almanac.com/humor4.shtml>

Name: _____

Date: _____

Student Performance Checklist:	Day 1		Day 2		Day 3	
	You	Listener*	You	Listener*	You	Listener*
Accurately read the passage 3–5 times.						
Read with appropriate phrasing and pausing.							
Read with appropriate expression.						
Read articulately at a good pace, and an audible volume.						

*Adult or peer

Self-reflection: What choices did you make when deciding how to read this passage, and why? What would you like to improve on or try differently next time? (*Thoughtfully answer these questions on this paper.*)

Handout 2B: Frayer Model

Directions: Working with a partner, complete the Frayer Model for the word *peculiar*.

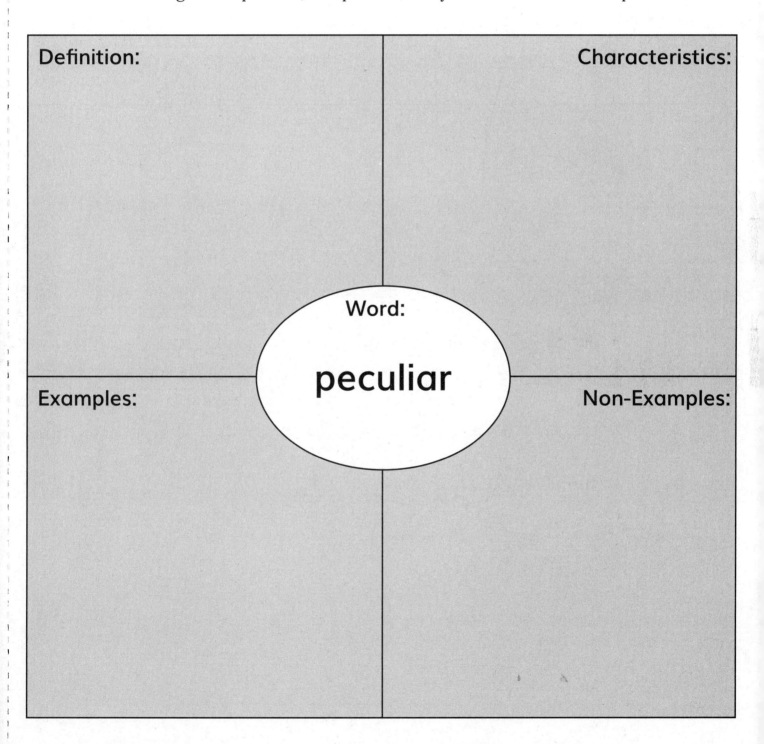

Handout 3A: "Who's on First?"

Directions: Read the skit "Who's on First?" Highlight the names of the baseball players on Abbott's team. (Hint: There are eight!) Then, in the right column, explain how the players' names cause confusion and misunderstanding between Abbott and Costello.

	"Who's on First?" by Bud Abbott and Lou Costello	Explain how the players' names are causing confusion in this scene. How do the players' names cause Abbott and Costello to misunderstand each other?
1	Abbott: Well Costello, I'm going to New York with you. You know Bucky Harris, the Yankees' manager, gave me a job as coach for as long as you're on the team.	
	Costello: Look Abbott, if you're the coach, you must know all the players.	
	Abbott: I certainly do.	
	Costello: Well you know I've never met the guys. So you'll have to tell me their names, and then I'll know who's playing on the team.	
5	Abbott: Oh, I'll tell you their names, but you know it seems to me they give these ball players now-a-days very peculiar names.	
	Costello: You mean funny names?	
	Abbott: Strange names, pet names...Well, let's see, we have on the bags, Who's on first, What's on second, I Don't Know is on third...	
	Costello: That's what I want to find out.	
	Abbott: I say Who's on first, What's on second, I Don't Know's on third.	

	Explain how the players' names are causing confusion in this scene. How do the players' names cause Abbott and Costello to misunderstand each other?

10 Costello: Are you the manager?

Abbott: Yes.

Costello: You gonna be the coach too?

Abbott: Yes.

Costello: And you don't know the fellows' names

15 Abbott: Well I should.

Costello: Well then who's on first?

Abbott: Yes.

Costello: I mean the fellow's name.

Abbott: Who.

20 Costello: The guy on first.

Abbott: Who.

Costello: The first baseman.

Abbott: Who.

Costello: The guy playing...

		Explain how the players' names are causing confusion in this scene. How do the players' names cause Abbott and Costello to misunderstand each other?	
25 Abbott: Who is on first! Costello: I'm asking YOU who's on first. Abbott: That's the man's name. Costello: That's who's name? Abbott: Yes.	30 Costello: Well go ahead and tell me. Abbott: That's it. Costello: That's who? Abbott: Yes. (PAUSE)	49 Costello: Look, all I wanna know is when you sign up the first baseman, how does he sign his name? 50 Abbott: Who. Costello: The guy. Abbott: Who. Costello: How does he sign... Abbott: That's how he signs it. 55 Costello: Who? Abbott: Yes. (PAUSE)	

	Explain how the players' names are causing confusion in this scene. How do the players' names cause Abbott and Costello to misunderstand each other?
69 70 75 80	Costello: What's the guy's name on first base? Abbott: No. What is on second. Costello: I'm not asking you who's on second. Abbott: Who's on first. Costello: I don't know. Abbott: He's on third, we're not talking about him. Costello: Now how did I get on third base? Abbott: Why you mentioned his name. Costello: If I mentioned the third baseman's name, who did I say is playing third? Abbott: No. Who's playing first. Costello: What's on first? Abbott: What's on second. Costello: I don't know. Abbott: He's on third. Costello: There I go, back on third again! (PAUSE)

		Explain how the players' names are causing confusion in this scene. How do the players' names cause Abbott and Costello to misunderstand each other?		Explain how the players' names are causing confusion in this scene. How do the players' names cause Abbott and Costello to misunderstand each other?
94	Costello: Look, you gotta outfield?		108	Costello: The left fielder's name?
95	Abbott: Sure.			Abbott: Why.
	Costello: The left fielder's name?		110	Costello: Because!
	Abbott: Why.			Abbott: Oh, he's centerfield.
	Costello: I just thought I'd ask you.			(PAUSE)
	Abbott: Well, I just thought I'd tell ya.			
100	Costello: Then tell me who's playing left field.			
	Abbott: Who's playing first.			
	Costello: I'm not... stay out of the infield! I want to know what's the guy's name in left field?			
	Abbott: No, What is on second.			
	Costello: I'm not asking you who's on second.			
105	Abbott: Who's on first!			
	Costello: I don't know.			
	Abbott & Costello Together: Third base! (PAUSE)			

Explain how the players' names are causing confusion in this scene. How do the players' names cause Abbott and Costello to misunderstand each other?		Explain how the players' names are causing confusion in this scene. How do the players' names cause Abbott and Costello to misunderstand each other?
	Costello: Look, You gotta pitcher on this team? Abbott: Sure. Costello: The pitcher's name?	
115	Abbott: Tomorrow. Costello: You don't want to tell me today? Abbott: I'm telling you now. Costello: Then go ahead. Abbott: Tomorrow! 120 Costello: What time? Abbott: What time what? Costello: What time tomorrow are you gonna tell me who's pitching? Abbott: Now listen. Who is not pitching. Costello: I'll break your arm, if you say who's on first! I want to know what's the pitcher's name? 125 Abbott: What's on second. Costello: I don't know. Abbott & Costello Together: Third base! (PAUSE)	
	Costello: Gotta a catcher? Abbott: Certainly.	

130	Costello: The catcher's name? Abbott: Today. Costello: Today, and tomorrow's pitching. Abbott: Now you've got it. Costello: All we got is a couple of days on the team. (PAUSE)	
135	Costello: You know I'm a catcher too. Abbott: So they tell me. Costello: I get behind the plate to do some fancy catching, Tomorrow's pitching on my team and a heavy hitter gets up. Now the heavy hitter bunts the ball. When he bunts the ball, me, being a good catcher, I'm gonna throw the guy out at first base. So I pick up the ball and throw it to who? Abbott: Now that's the first thing you've said right. Costello: I don't even know what I'm talking about! (PAUSE)	Explain how the players' names are causing confusion in this scene. How do the players' names cause Abbott and Costello to misunderstand each other?
140	Abbott: That's all you have to do. Costello: Is to throw the ball to first base. Abbott: Yes! Costello: Now who's got it? Abbott: Naturally. (PAUSE)	Explain how the players' names are causing confusion in this scene. How do the players' names cause Abbott and Costello to misunderstand each other?

Name: _____

Date: _____

Explain how the players' names are causing confusion in this scene. How do the players' names cause Abbott and Costello to misunderstand each other?	

145 Costello: Look, if I throw the ball to first base, somebody's gotta get it. Now who has it?

Abbott: Naturally.

Costello: Who?

Abbott: Naturally.

Costello: Naturally?

150 Abbott: Naturally.

Costello: So I pick up the ball and I throw it to Naturally.

Abbott: No you don't, you throw the ball to Who.

Costello: Naturally.

Abbott: That's different.

155 Costello: That's what I said.

Abbott: You're not saying it...

Costello: I throw the ball to Naturally.

Abbott: You throw it to Who.

Costello: Naturally.

160 Abbott: That's it.

Costello: That's what I said!

Abbott: You ask me.

Costello: I throw the ball to who?

Abbott: Naturally.

	Explain how the players' names are causing confusion in this scene. How do the players' names cause Abbott and Costello to misunderstand each other?

165 Costello: Now you ask me.

Abbott: You throw the ball to Who?

Costello: Naturally.

Abbott: That's it.

Costello: Same as you! Same as YOU! I throw the ball to who. Whoever it is drops the ball and the guy runs to second. Who picks up the ball and throws it to What. What throws it to I Don't Know. I Don't Know throws it back to Tomorrow, Triple play. Another guy gets up and hits a long fly ball to Because. Why? I don't know! He's on third and I don't give a darn!

170 Abbott: What?

Costello: I said I don't give a darn!

Abbott: Oh, that's our shortstop.

Name: _____

Date: _____

Handout 4A: Speaking and Listening Style Checklist

Directions: Evaluate your participation and/or speaking performance by marking + for "yes" and ∆ for "not yet" in the appropriate boxes in the "Self" column.

Grade 5 Speaking and Listening Style Checklist			
	Self +/ ∆	Peer +/ ∆	Teacher +/ ∆
I choose strong, precise words to express my ideas and feelings clearly.			
I speak in a clear voice.			
I speak at a pace at which I can be understood by my audience.			
I adjust my speaking voice–including my volume, pitch, and inflection–as appropriate for my purpose and audience.			
I use body language–including eye contact, good posture, gestures, facial expression–as appropriate for my purpose and audience.			
I adjust my speech to the context–for example, using my formal speaking voice for academic conversations or reading with expression for a literary read-aloud or performance.			
*When appropriate, I use visuals, sound, or other multimedia effects to add detail to my spoken descriptions.			
Total number of +'s:			

*This indicator will be assessed more formally in Module 4, when students present formal research. It is included here as an optional criterion, as there are opportunities to practice this in the context of character illustrations to accompany written "snapshots" for Focusing Question Task 2, or through extension activities.

Name: _____

Date: _____

Handout 5A: Fluency Homework

Directions:
1. Day 1: Read the text carefully and annotate to help you read fluently.
2. Each day:
   a. Practice reading the text three to five times.
   b. Evaluate your progress by placing a ✓+, ✓, or ✓- in each unshaded box.
   c. Ask someone (adult or peer) to listen and evaluate you as well.
3. Last day: Respond to the self-reflection questions.

There was once a boy named Milo who didn't know what to do with himself—not just sometimes, but always.

When he was in school he longed to be out, and when he was out he longed to be in. On the way home he thought about coming home, and coming home he thought about going. Wherever he was he wished he were somewhere else, and when he got there he wondered why he'd bothered. Nothing really interested him—least of all the things that should have.

"It seems to me that almost everything is a waste of time," he remarked one day as he walked dejectedly home from school. "I can't see the point in learning to solve useless problems, or subtracting turnips from turnips, or knowing where Ethiopia is or how to spell February." And, since no one bothered to explain otherwise, he regarded the process of seeking knowledge as the greatest waste of time of all.

Juster, Norton. *The Phantom Tollbooth*. New York: Random House, 1961. Print.

Name: _____

Date: _____

Student Performance Checklist:	Day 1		Day 2		Day 3	
	You	Listener*	You	Listener*	You	Listener*
Accurately read the passage 3–5 times.						
Read with appropriate phrasing and pausing.						
Read with appropriate expression.						
Read articulately at a good pace, and an audible volume.						

*Adult or peer

Self-reflection: What choices did you make when deciding how to read this passage, and why? What would you like to improve on or try differently next time? (*Thoughtfully answer these questions on this paper.*)

Name: _____

Date: _____

Handout 6A: Setting and Character Analysis Chart

Directions: Complete each row of the chart below to help you understand the meaning (and wordplay!) of a place or character name in *The Phantom Tollbooth*.

Setting or Character Name		
Description How does the author describe this setting or character? (For characters, consider his or her looks, words, and actions.) Include direct quotations or paraphrasing.		
Illustration What does the illustration of this place or character show? How does it add to your understanding of the place or character?		
Literal Meaning Based on the description and illustration, infer the meaning of the setting's or character's name. Verify the meaning using a dictionary or teacher-provided definition.	My definition:	Actual definition:
Wordplay How is this setting's or character's name an example of wordplay? Explain how the meaning of the place or character name is revealed through the author's description.		

Name: _____

Date: _____

Handout 6B: Precise Words

Directions: Read each sentence below. Choose the word from the list that best fits the context of the sentence. Use each word only once. If a word needs to be past tense, add a –d or an –ed.

meditate	presume	reason	speculate	surmise

1. The later it got, the harder it was to _____, so I put my math homework away until morning.

2. He _____ his teacher would give him extra time to complete his project since he had been sick.

3. Since I had no facts, I could only _____ about my sister's motives.

4. I _____ that Grandma is staying for a few weeks since she brought several suitcases with her.

5. "Are you going to stand there and _____ about jumping off the diving board, or are you going to jump?" teased my cousin.

Handout 8A: Observe-Infer-Wonder Chart

Name: _____

Date: _____

Directions: Read over the spoken words, of the advisors, from pages 38–44. For each clip of the advisors' conversation with Milo, record your observations and inferences. You may also record anything you wonder about the king's advisors or about Dictionopolis in the "I Wonder" column.

What the King's Advisors Say	I Observe…	I Infer…	I Wonder…
	Example: I observe that they all seem to say basically the same thing, but each uses a different synonym.	*Example:* I infer that the king's advisors like using lots of different words! They seem to be obsessed with words.	*Example:* I wonder, will every interaction Milo has with people in Dictionopolis be so confusing?
"Greetings!" "Salutations!" "Welcome!" "Good afternoon!" "Hello!" (38)			
"You see," continued the minister, bowing thankfully to the duke, "Dictionopolis is the place where all the words in the world come from. They're grown right here in our orchards." (42)			
"We're not interested in making sense; it's not our job," scolded the first. "Besides," explained the second, "one word is as good as another—so why not use them all?" "Then you don't have to choose which one is right," advised the third. "Besides," sighed the fourth, "if one is right, then ten are ten times as right." (40)			

Name: _____

Date: _____

"Our job," said the count, "is to see that all the words sold are proper ones, for it wouldn't do to sell someone a word that had no meaning or didn't exist at all." (42)	"But we never choose which ones to use," explained the earl as they walked toward the market stalls, "for as long as they mean what they mean to mean we don't care if they make sense or nonsense." (43)	"You see," cautioned the count, "you must pick your words very carefully and be sure to say just what you intend to say." (44)

Handout 8C: Precise Words

Directions: Read the passage below adapted from pages 45–46 of *The Phantom Tollbooth*. Replace the imprecise words, such as *lots*, *vehicles*, *things*, *people*, *places*, and *stuff*, with precise words. Draw a line through the imprecise words and phrases and write more precise, descriptive words and phrases above them.

"Come," he shouted. "Let's see the market. It looks very exciting."

Indeed it was. Milo saw people doing lots of things. Vehicles came into the market from other places, and other vehicles were there too. Things were in the vehicles, and there were people doing lots of different stuff. But above all the noise of the crowd could be heard people loudly saying things.

So many words and so many people! They were from lots of places, and they were all busy doing stuff. There seemed to be no end to all the things going on.

G5 > M2 > Handout 9A • WIT & WISDOM™

Name: _____

Date: _____

Handout 9A: Painting Analysis Chart

Directions: For each painting, answer the questions in the chart below.

Painting	What everyday objects do you see in this painting?	How have these everyday objects been changed to seem surreal, or dream-like?	How does the arrangement or placement of objects make them appear surreal?	What do you notice about the figure in the center on the ground?
Painting by Salvador Dalí				
Painting by René Magritte				

G5 > M2 > Handout 9A • WIT & WISDOM™

Name: _____

Date: _____

Directions: Now examine the groups of objects listed in the chart below, and then answer the questions for each group of objects. Add any other surprising juxtapositions you notice in the blank rows.

Painting	Objects	What do you notice about the juxtaposition? How do the objects compare? Contrast?
Salvador Dalí	ants; pocket watch (time piece)	
	clock; creature's profile (center of painting)	
	the two rectangular prisms	
	clock folded over the tree branch	
René Magritte	train; fireplace	
	mirror; fireplace	
	train; clock	

Handout 9B: Setting Snapshot

Directions: Read the setting snapshot "Welcome to Abandon." Then, reread and annotate sensory language the writer uses to help you visualize this imaginary place called "Abandon." Use the following annotation symbols: see (S); hear (H); smell (Sm); taste (T); feel/touch (F).

Welcome to Abandon

A green sign announced "Welcome to the Town of Abandon." Milo and Tock peered curiously at their surroundings as their little car puttered through the small town. The road was only partially paved and filled with potholes. Next to a large pothole sat an orange sign that read, "Warning: Road work in progress, or maybe not." In the center of town, half of the buildings appeared to be under construction. Some buildings didn't have roofs. Others were missing entire walls! An entire construction crew napped soundly on the sidewalk outside one half-completed building. Through the window of a diner, Milo spied plates of half-eaten scrambled eggs and toast left on red-and-white checkered tabletops. A girl delivering newspapers on her bicycle tossed one into their moving vehicle. Then, she ditched her newspaper bag on the curb and pedaled off, whistling cheerfully. Tock unrolled the paper and growled, "Why, these stories are only half-written! How are we supposed to find out what's going on around here?" Milo shrugged and turned to watch a group of children playing baseball in a field. With a loud crack!, the batter smacked the ball high into the air. The other players watched the ball sail upwards, tossed off their mitts, and wandered off in different directions. Milo stared after them, confused, and scratched his head. Just past the center of town, Milo and Tock passed a building whose sign read, in peeling paint, "Abandon Elementary School: If at first you don't succeed, you might as well give up

Handout 10A: "Tired" Words and Some Punchier Alternatives

Directions: In the tables below, you'll find more vivid words to replace the tired, overused words along the top. Use these options to spice up your writing! Add words to the charts as you think of them.

said	went	walked	looked
expressed	moved	skipped	glanced
uttered	proceeded	strolled	gazed
pleaded	advanced	plodded	stared
agreed	ambled	hiked	gaped
demanded	crept	trudged	peered
mumbled	sped	stomped	considered
hollered	hurried	strode	viewed
sighed	vanished	marched	examined
questioned			inspected
replied			
remembered			
promised			

Name: _____

Date: _____

helped	thought	happy	sad
assisted	pondered	cheerful	depressed
aided	reflected	joyful	miserable
eased	deliberated	carefree	down
alleviated	contemplated	lighthearted	glum
improved	recalled	delighted	gloomy
lessened	imagined	pleased	heartbroken

okay	good/great	really	important
all right	delightful	truly	significant
very well	lovely	honestly	major
fair enough	pleasant	genuinely	momentous
acceptable	passionate		key
	enthusiastic		essential

Handout 11A: Character Snapshot

Directions: Read the following snapshot about the mayor of the town of Abandon, Mayor McQuitter, and think about how the author shows readers this character's traits, or personality. Then, reread and annotate details about Mayor McQuitter's looks, words, and actions that helped you infer her traits.

Meet Mayor McQuitter

Milo and Tock peered through the mayor's office doorway. Papers littered the mayor's desk and surrounding floor, as if a great gust of wind had swept in and scattered them. A gold nameplate that read "Mayor McQuitter" sat on the desk. Behind it, they glimpsed a pair of half-laced sneakers propped up on the desk. Two legs, each clad in a different color stocking, grew out of the sneakers and disappeared under a long sweater. One of the town's newspapers, full of half-written stories, was spread across the mayor's head. Loud snores made the paper rise and fall over the mayor's face. "Ahem," Milo politely cleared his throat to get the mayor's attention. On the third try, a head full of thick black curls popped up

Name: _____

Date: _____

from beneath the newspaper. "Oh, hello there. Who are you, please? Oh, never mind, what can I do for…huh–" Mayor McQuitter stopped mid-sentence and began shuffling through papers on her desk. She scanned one, tossed it, then scanned another and tossed it, too.

"So many new project proposals! Let's start them all, I say! We'll never finish them anyway. Now who did you say you…Have you seen my assistant?" Mayor McQuitter hopped up, set a teapot to boil on the small stove behind her, and waltzed out the door past Milo and Tock.

Name: _____

Date: _____

Handout 12A: Frayer Model

Directions: Create a Frayer Model for the word *abandon*. Include the definition of this word, characteristics, examples, and nonexamples.

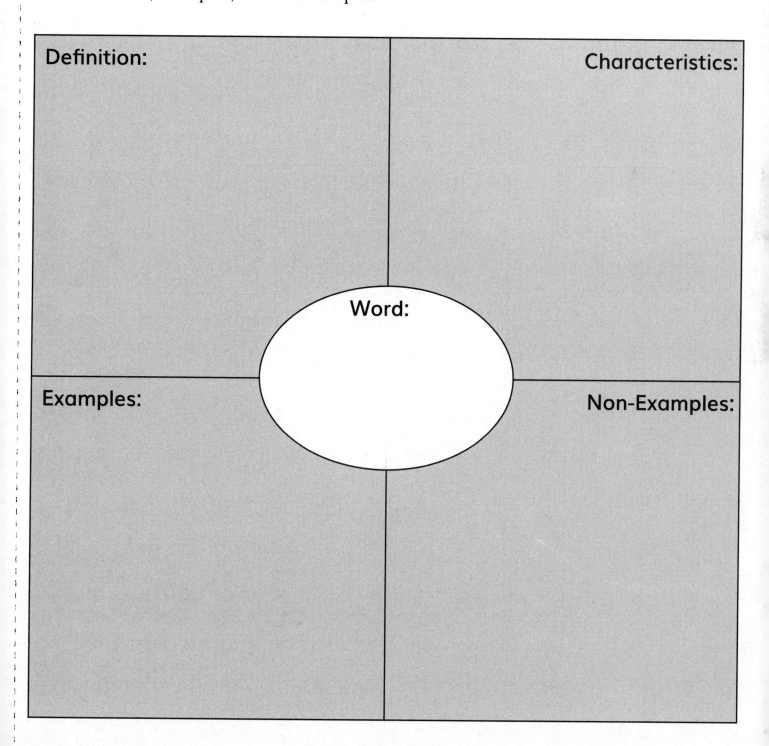

Name: _____

Date: _____

Handout 12B: Character Snapshot Planner

Directions: Follow the steps below for Parts I and II to help you develop your character from Abandon Elementary School. Use the planner to help you organize your ideas.

Part I:

First, decide which character you want to write about: a student, teacher, principal, or other school employee of Abandon Elementary School. Record ideas for your character's name, related to the word *abandon*. Use the Frayer Model for *abandon* on Handout 12A to help you come up with ideas for a name.

Now, think about your inner qualities, or his/her character's traits, or personality. What is he/she like? What are his/her beliefs and attitude about school and about learning? Remember, your character's inner qualities should relate to the meaning of the word *abandon*.

Next, think about your character's outer qualities. Describe his or her physical characteristics, including gender, age, and physical appearance. How might you reinforce the wordplay of your character's name through his/her outer qualities?

My character is:
- ☐ A student
- ☐ A teacher
- ☐ The principal
- ☐ Another school employee: _____

Ideas for my character's name, related to the word *abandon*, include:

Inner Qualities	Outer Qualities
Describe your character's traits, or personality. What are his/her beliefs and attitude about school and about learning? How do they relate to the meaning of abandon?	Describe his/her physical characteristics, including gender, age, and physical appearance. How will you reinforce the wordplay of your character's name in your description of his/her appearance?

Name: _____

Date: _____

Part II: Remember, actions and words reveal character. How will you <u>show</u>, rather than <u>tell</u> your reader about your character, through his/her actions and words?

Actions	Words
How can you show what your character is like through his/her actions? Describe how he/she might behave or act in a way that reveals his/her traits—especially his/her attitude and beliefs about school and learning.	How can you show what your character is like through his/her words? What kinds of things might this character say that reveal his/her attitude and beliefs about school and learning?

Name: _____

Date: _____

Handout 13A: Oral Story Map

Directions: Use the sentence frames on this story map to help you orally organize and summarize Faintly Macabre's story of Rhyme and Reason.

Faintly Macabre's Story of Rhyme and Reason

Setting:	Characters: Describe each of the following characters, including their roles in the kingdom.
This story takes place…	*The prince/King of Wisdom is…*
Before the young prince arrived, this place was….	*King Azaz is…*
	The Mathemagician is…
After the young prince established his kingdom, this place became…	*The Princesses Rhyme and Reason are…*

Name: _____

Date: _____

Action/Problem: Briefly describe the events that led to the division in the kingdom and the imprisonment of Rhyme and Reason.

First…

Next…

Then…

After that…

Finally, the Princesses Rhyme and Reason were banished to the Castle in the Air because…

Ending: Briefly describe what happened in the Kingdom of Wisdom as a result of Rhyme and Reason's banishment.

After Rhyme and Reason were banished to the Castle in the Air, the Kingdom of Wisdom…

Nuggets of Wisdom: What can the characters—and Milo—learn from the story of Rhyme and Reason and their banishment from the Kingdom of Wisdom? (Think about how their banishment affected the kingdom.)

The story of Rhyme and Reason's banishment can serve as a lesson to teach Milo and the people in the Kingdom of Wisdom…

Handout 13B: Fluency Homework

Directions:
1. Day 1: Read the text carefully and annotate to help you read fluently.
2. Each day:
    a. Practice reading the text three to five times.
    b. Evaluate your progress by placing a ✓+, ✓, or ✓- in each unshaded box.
    c. Ask someone (adult or peer) to listen and evaluate you as well.
3. Last day: Respond to the self-reflection questions.

Everyone loved the princesses because of their great beauty, their gentle ways, and their ability to settle all controversies fairly and reasonably. People with problems or grievances or arguments came from all over the land to seek advice, and even the two brothers, who by this time were fighting continuously, often called upon them to help decide matters of state. It was said by everyone that "Rhyme and Reason answer all problems."

As the years passed, the two brothers grew farther and farther apart and their separate kingdoms became richer and grander. Their disputes, however, became more and more difficult to reconcile. But always, with patience and love, the princesses set things right.

Juster, Norton. *The Phantom Tollbooth*. New York: Random House, 1961. Print.

Name: _____

Date: _____

Student Performance Checklist:	Day 1		Day 2		Day 3	
	You	Listener*	You	Listener*	You	Listener*
Accurately read the passage 3-5 times.						
Read with appropriate phrasing and pausing.						
Read with appropriate expression.						
Read articulately at a good pace, and an audible volume.						

*Adult or peer

Self-reflection: What choices did you make when deciding how to read this passage, and why? What would you like to improve on or try differently next time? (*Thoughtfully answer these questions on this paper.*)

Handout 14A: Think-Pair-Square-Share with Adages

Name: _____

Date: _____

Directions: In the first column, write the adage or proverb. In the second column, write what you think it means. In the third column, write what your partner thinks it means. In the next column, write what your new partner thinks it means. In the last column, your group of four will decide the meaning you will share with the class.

What is the adage or proverb?	THINK: What do I think it means, and why?	PAIR: What does my partner think it means, and why?	SQUARE: What does my new partner think it means, and why?	SHARE: What will we share?
Don't make mountains out of molehills.	I think it means do not make something out of nothing because mountains are big and molehills are small.			Don't cause something simple to seem much more difficult than it is.
Make hay while the sun shines.				
Leave no stone unturned.				

G5 > M2 > Handout 14A • WIT & WISDOM™

Copyright © 2016 Great Minds®

Name: _____

Date: _____

Handout 15A: Focusing Question Task 2 Checklist

Directions: Use this checklist to help you assess and revise your writing. Mark + for "yes" and Δ for "not yet." You may ask someone (adult or peer) to evaluate your writing as well.

Character Snapshot Writing Checklist	Self +/ Δ	Peer +/ Δ	Teacher +/ Δ
Reading Comprehension			
• I create a character who is a student, teacher, principal, or other school employee at the imaginary "Abandon Elementary School."			
• My character's name and snapshot involves a play on meaning of *abandon*.			
• Through my snapshot, I convey my character's attitude and beliefs about school and learning, related to the meaning of *abandon*.			
Structure			
• In my lead, I quickly establish: 　o characters, including Milo and my character; 　o the setting, Abandon Elementary School; 　o a situation, or scene, in which Milo meets my character.			
• I organize my events in a natural order.			
• I use transitions to tie details and events together.			
Development			
• I use description and at least one line of dialogue to show my character's actions and words and reveal his/her attitude and beliefs.			
• I use concrete and sensory details to help my reader visualize my character and reinforce the wordplay of his/her name.			

Name:

Date:

Style			
• My writing style is appropriate for the audience.			
• I choose precise words—including vivid verbs; concrete, or specific details; and prepositional phrases—to add detail to my writing and "show-not-tell."			
Conventions			
• I use proper capitalization, punctuation, and spelling.			
Writing Process			

• I revise my snapshot to:
   o replace tired, overused verbs with vivid verbs that "pack a punch";
   o replace imprecise words with concrete, specific details;
   o add detail using prepositional phrases.			

Total number of +'s:			

Handout 16A: Plot Flowcharts

Directions: After reviewing the parts of a plot flowchart, fill in examples of each part of the plot using *Thunder Rolling in the Mountains*.

Traditional Plot Flowchart

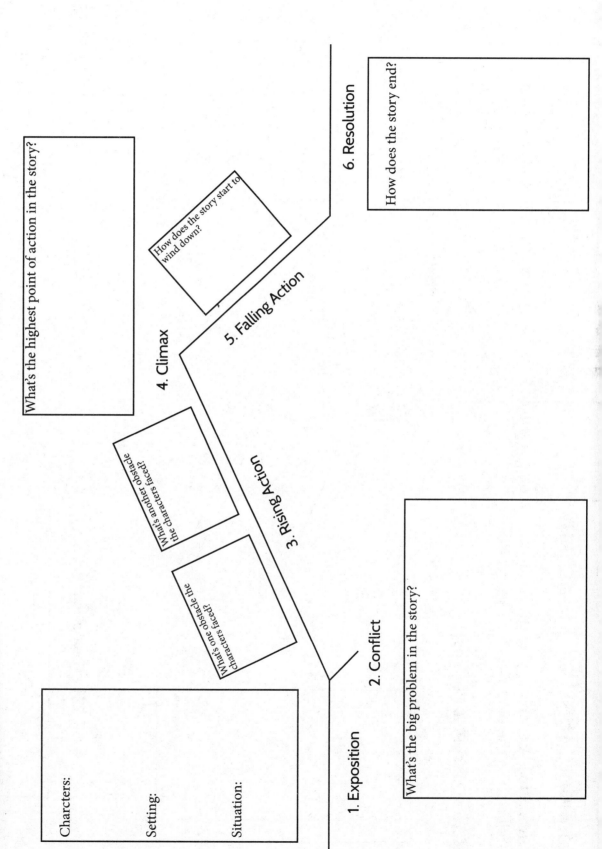

Handout 16A: Plot Flowcharts

Directions: After reviewing the parts of a hero's quest plot flowchart, record notes from *The Phantom Tollbooth* as the plot of the story develops.

Hero's Quest Plot Flowchart

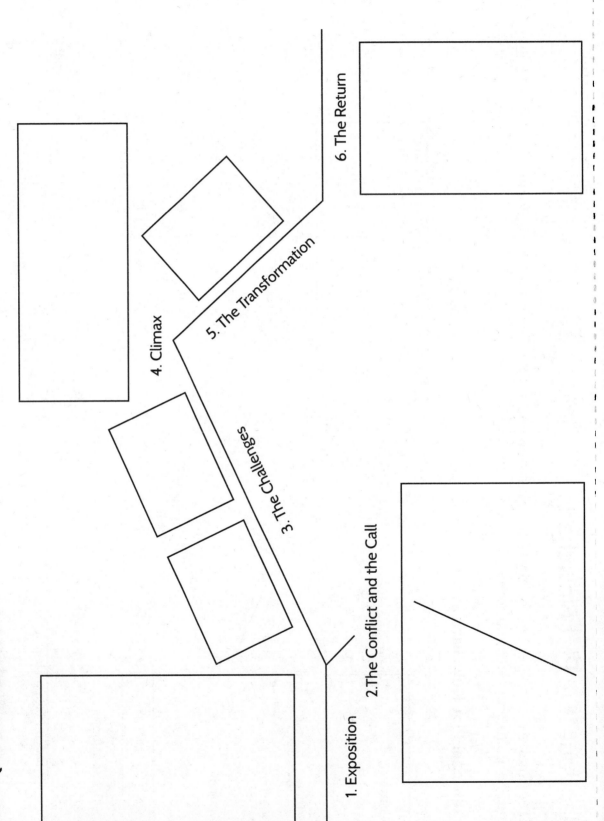

1. Exposition
2. The Conflict and the Call
3. The Challenges
4. Climax
5. The Transformation
6. The Return

Handout 16B: Fluency Homework

Directions:
1. Day 1: Read the text carefully and annotate to help you read fluently.
2. Each day:
    a. Practice reading the text three to five times.
    b. Evaluate your progress by placing a ✓+, ✓, or ✓- in each unshaded box.
    c. Ask someone (adult or peer) to listen and evaluate you as well.
3. Last day: Respond to the self-reflection questions.

"Dictionopolis will always be grateful, my boy," interrupted the king, throwing one arm around Milo and patting Tock with the other. "You will face many dangers on your journey, but fear not, for I have brought you this for your protection."

He drew from inside his cape a small heavy box about the size of a schoolbook and handed it ceremoniously to Milo.

"In this box are all the words I know," he said. "Most of them you will never need, some you will use constantly, but with them you may ask all the questions which have never been answered and answer all the questions which have never been asked. All the great books of the past and all the ones yet to come are made with these words. With them there is no obstacle you cannot overcome. All you must learn to do is use them well and in the right places."

Juster, Norton. *The Phantom Tollbooth*. New York: Random House, 1961. Print.

Name: _____

Date: _____

Student Performance Checklist:	Day 1		Day 2		Day 3	
	You	Listener*	You	Listener*	You	Listener*
Accurately read the passage 3–5 times.						
Read with appropriate phrasing and pausing.						
Read with appropriate expression.						
Read articulately at a good pace, and an audible volume.						

*Adult or peer

Self-reflection: What choices did you make when deciding how to read this passage, and why? What would you like to improve on or try differently next time? (*Thoughtfully answer these questions on this paper.*)

Name: _____

Date: _____

Handout 16C: Synonym Quest

Directions: Read the passage assigned to your group. Select two or three words that you do not know and look them up in a thesaurus. Replace the unknown word with a familiar synonym by writing the synonym above the unknown word. Then, whisper-read the passage in your group.

Passage 1, pages 96–97:

"All that he would have to do," continued the worried bug, "is travel through miles of harrowing and hazardous countryside, into unknown valleys and uncharted forests, past yawning chasms and trackless wastes, until he reached Digitopolis (if, of course, he ever reached there). Then he would have to persuade the Mathemagician to agree to release the little princesses—and, of course, he'd never agree to agree to anything that you agreed with. And, anyway, if he did, you certainly wouldn't agree to it."

Name: _____

Date: _____

Passage 2, page 97:

"From there it's a simple matter of entering the Mountains of Ignorance, full of perilous pitfalls and ominous overtones—a land to which many venture but few return, and whose evil demons slither slowly from peak to peak in search of prey. Then an effortless climb up a two-thousand-step circular stairway without railings in a high wind at night (for in those mountains it is always night) to the Castle in the Air."

Passage 3, page 97:

He paused momentarily for breath, then began again.

"After a pleasant chat with the princesses, all that remains is a leisurely ride back through those chaotic crags whose frightening fiends have sworn to tear any intruder limb from limb and devour him down to his belt buckle.

"And, finally, after the long ride back, a triumphal parade (if, of course, there is anything left to parade) followed by hot chocolate and cookies for everyone." The Humbug bowed low and sat down once again, very pleased with himself.

Name: _____

Date: _____

Handout 17A: ESCAPE Structure for Narrative Stories

Directions: Use the "ESCAPE" structure for narrative stories to help you think about individual episodes in *The Phantom Tollbooth* and to help you think about how you might use this structure in your own narrative episode.

		Narrative Episodes in *The Phantom Tollbooth*
E	**Establish** – Establish a situation to orient your reader and provide context.	
S	**Setting** – Establish a setting. Where and when does the story take place?	
C	**Characters** – Establish characters. Who is the story about, and what are they like?	
A	**Action** – What events happen, and how do the characters respond?	
P	**Problem** – What conflict does the main character face?	
E	**Ending** – How does the story end? How is the conflict resolved?	

Remember, a good story captures readers' interest and pulls them in. As a writer of stories, your job is to make your readers ESCAPE into your story! Check to make sure your story includes all of the elements of ESCAPE.

Handout 18A: Exploded Moment Model

Directions: Read the following "exploded moment" model to help you plan your own exploded moment.

The Abandoned Bridge

1. Mayor McQuitter waved for Milo, Tock, and the Humbug to follow her out of her office.

2. "I'm going to meet with the construction crew building the bridge over the Persistence River. They have a problem," Mayor McQuitter said as Milo, Tock, and the Humbug ran to catch up.

3. "We wanted to talk to you about that," Milo called. "We're on our way to Digitopolis, but the road ended. The bridge doesn't cross the river the whole way. Is there another way over the Persistence?"

4. "Nope, no other way, unless…" Instead of finishing her thought, she began to tell them more about the town of Abandon.

5. "Oh, here we are!" she exclaimed.

6. A crew of workers sat beside the river, sipping coffee. Behind them, Milo glimpsed wooden beams piled up on the banks of the raging river. Milo and the others stood back as the mayor walked over to the crew. They spoke briefly. The mayor smiled, shrugged, and then returned.

7. "Problem solved!" the mayor called out.

8. "Great news! When will the bridge be done?" Milo asked hopefully.

9. "Completed? No. Too many problems. We're throwing in the towel!" Mayor McQuitter replied.

10. "Oh," said Milo. "That doesn't make much sense. Surely the problems can be solved. Do you mind me asking what the problems are?"

11. The mayor blew her cheeks up like a balloon and let out a breath. "Well, to start with, the wooden beams we cut are too long, and…Well, you get the idea."

12. "No, not really," Milo began. "Um, couldn't you cut the beams down to the correct size, rather than quit everything? That seems like only a little problem, really."

Name: _____

Date: _____

13   The mayor wrinkled her nose. "Young man, there is no use wasting energy trying to solve these problems. It's easier to give up and move on to something else! Ever since Rhyme and Reason were banished from the kingdom, this way has worked well for us."

14   Milo noticed this was the clearest thought the mayor had said since they'd met. "Pardon me, I just thought–" he began.

15   "You may keep your thinking to yourself, thank you. Now, crossing Persistence is out of the question. I recommend you head out of town the same way you came. It was very nice to…" but the mayor had already walked away.

16   Milo, Tock, and the Humbug exchanged a meaningful look. As they went off in search of their car, Milo thought to himself, "How silly to give up whenever a problem seems too hard. They'll never accomplish anything around here!" He felt more eager than ever to follow through on his mission to rescue Rhyme and Reason.

Name: _____

Date: _____

Handout 19B: Exploded Moment Planner

Directions: In the following boxes, brainstorm ideas for your exploded moment with Milo and your character from Focusing Question Task 2. Be sure your ideas include wordplay with ideas related to your character's name and the meaning of *abandon*.

Establish Setting, Characters, and Situation

Setting

Your story takes place at Abandon Elementary. Where specifically in the school are Milo and your character going to interact?

Wordplay: Think about what your setting looks and sounds like and how it might relate to the meaning of abandon.

Characters

Write the name of the character you developed for Focusing Question Task 2, who Milo will interact with in this scene:

Wordplay: How will you depict your character in a way that illuminates the meaning of his or her name and abandon? Think about how your character looks, acts, and talks, as well as his/her traits and beliefs about school and learning. (Draw on details of your character from Focusing Question Task 2!)

Name: _____

Date: _____

Situation

Describe the situation, or what is going on, when Milo encounters this character in your scene. (Remember, Milo needs directions out of Abandon.)

Action/Problem

Describe the interaction between Milo and your character in this scene. How will the character challenge Milo's ideas about school and learning in this scene? How will the characters respond to each other's ideas to show their conflicting ideas?

Wordplay: How do your character's beliefs about school and learning relate to his or her name and the meaning of abandon?

Name: _____

Date: _____

Ending

How will your story end? How will you reveal a new learning or understanding that Milo gains as a result of his interaction with this character?

Wordplay: Think about the lesson or understanding that Milo gains from his interaction with this character. How does that lesson relate to the ideas represented by the town and characters of Abandon?

Name: _____

Date: _____

Handout 19C: Fluency Homework

Directions:
1. Day 1: Read the text carefully and annotate to help you read fluently.
2. Each day:
   a. Practice reading the text three to five times.
   b. Evaluate your progress by placing a ✓+, ✓, or ✓- in each unshaded box.
   c. Ask someone (adult or peer) to listen and evaluate you as well.
3. Last day: Respond to the self-reflection questions.

"I'm sorry you can't stay longer," said Alec sadly. "There's so much more to see in the Forest of Sight. But I suppose there's a lot to see everywhere, if only you keep your eyes open."

They walked for a while, all silent in their thoughts, until they reached the car and Alec drew a fine telescope from his shirt and handed it to Milo.

"Carry this with you on your journey," he said softly, "for there is much worth noticing that often escapes the eye. Through it you can see everything from the tender moss in a sidewalk crack to the glow of the farthest star—and, most important of all, you can see things as they really are, not just as they seem to be. It's my gift to you."

Milo placed the telescope carefully in the glove compartment, and reached up to shake Alec by the hand. Then he stepped on the starter and, with his head full of strange new thoughts, drove out the far end of the forest.

Juster, Norton. *The Phantom Tollbooth*. New York: Random House, 1961. Print.

Name: _____

Date: _____

Student Performance Checklist:	Day 1		Day 2		Day 3		Day 4	
	You	Listener*	You	Listener*	You	Listener*	You	Listener*
Accurately read the passage 3–5 times.								
Read with appropriate phrasing and pausing.								
Read with appropriate expression.								
Read articulately at a good pace and an audible volume.								

*Adult or peer

Self-reflection: What choices did you make when deciding how to read this passage, and why? What would you like to improve on or try differently next time? (*Thoughtfully answer these questions on this paper.*)

Name: _____

Date: _____

Handout 20A: Dialogue Quest

Directions: Choose the challenges you'd like to face on your quest to gain knowledge about why dialogue is important in a text. Across the top, you'll see a place to keep track of the challenges you complete along the way, and how many of each challenge you are expected to do. You'll earn one point for each challenge successfully completed, and you'll need a total of six points. You can check off a challenge as you complete it by checking off the star in each box. Note that you don't have to complete every challenge to fulfill your mission on this quest.

Character Descriptions Row 1: _____ / 2	Background/Context Row 2: _____ / 1	Conflicting Ideas Row 3: _____ / 3	Wordplay with Ideas Row 4: _____ / 1

Character Descriptions: Dr. Dischord, page 133
How do we learn what Dischord is like from dialogue?
From dialogue, we learn that…

Character Descriptions: DYNNE, page 139
How do we learn what DYNNE is like from dialogue?
From dialogue, we learn that…

Background/Context, pages 137–38
How do we learn about the context of Dr. Dischord's popularity from dialogue?
From dialogue, we learn that Dr. Dischord became popular…

G5 > M2 > Handout 20A • WIT & WISDOM™

Name: _____

Date: _____

Conflicting Ideas, page 137	**Conflicting Ideas, pages 138**	**Conflicting Ideas, page 142**
How do we learn from dialogue about how Milo's ideas conflict with Dr. Dischord's ideas? From dialogue, we learn that Milo…	*How do we learn from dialogue about how Milo's ideas conflict with Dr. Dischord's ideas?* From dialogue, we learn that Milo…	*How do we learn from dialogue about how Milo's ideas conflict with Dr. Dischord's ideas?* From dialogue, we learn that Milo…

Wordplay with Ideas, page 141	**Wordplay with Sounds, page 142**
How do we learn about the wordplay of din/DYNNE from dialogue? From dialogue, we learn that…	*How do we learn about the wordplay of sounds from dialogue?* From dialogue, we learn that…

Name: _____

Date: _____

Handout 21A: Story Map

Directions: Use this story map to organize and record notes about key elements in chapter 12 and pages 161–164 of chapter 13.

Setting: Describe the following settings. The Valley of Sound: The Soundkeeper's Fortress:	**Characters:** Describe the characters Milo encounters in this part of the story. Residents of the Valley of Sound: The Soundkeeper:

Action/Problem: Briefly desribe the action, or events, that happen in this episode, including the problem that Milo faces.

Ending: Briefly describe the outcome of events in this episode, including how the problem is resolved.

Name: _____

Date: _____

Nuggets of Wisdom: What does Milo learn from his experiences in the Valley of Sound? What knowledge or understanding does he gain?

How does this episode in the Valley of Sound represent a "turning point" for Milo's character? What change(s) do you see in Milo from the beginning of the story? Support your ideas with evidence from the story.

Name: _____

Date: _____

Handout 22A: Dialogue Planner

Directions: Think of an idea, related to school and learning, that Milo and the character you invented from the town of Abandon could disagree about. Then, think about each character's ideas, or beliefs, about this topic. Finally, draft sample dialogue lines that each character might say back and forth to each other.

1. The Disagreement Milo and my character could disagree about…	**2. The Purpose** The purpose, or point, of their conversation is …
3. Milo's Ideas In this conversation, Milo thinks…	**4. The Other Character's Ideas** However, my character thinks…

Wordplay Ideas/Phrases
How can you play with the meanings of the word abandon and your character's name (e.g., Mayor McQuitter) in their conversation?

Name: _____

Date: _____

Milo

My other character _____

G5 > M2 > Handout 22A • WIT & WISDOM™

Name: _____

Date: _____

Name:

Date:

Handout 22B: Conventions of Dialogue-Writing

Directions:
1. Read this passage.
2. Based on what you have learned about the conventions of dialogue, place the paragraph sign (¶) whenever a new paragraph is required.
3. Then, read through the passage again and underline or highlight dialogue, or characters' spoken words.
4. Based on what you have learned about the conventions of dialogue, add punctuation, including quotation marks, commas, and any necessary end punctuation.
5. Rewrite the paragraph in your Response Journals or on the back of this handout with proper formatting and punctuation. Remember to indent each new paragraph.

Mayor McQuitter waved for Milo, Tock, and the Humbug to follow her out of her office.

I'm going to meet with the construction crew building the bridge over the Persistence River. They have a problem Mayor McQuitter said as Milo, Tock, and the Humbug ran to catch up.

We wanted to talk to you about that Milo called. We're on our way to Digitopolis, but the road ended. The bridge doesn't cross the river the whole way. Is there another way over the Persistence? Nope no other way, unless… Instead of finishing her thought, she began to tell them more about the town of Abandon. Oh here we are! she exclaimed. A crew of workers sat beside the river, sipping coffee. Behind them, Milo glimpsed wooden beams piled up on the banks of the raging river. Milo and the others stood back as the mayor walked over to the crew. They spoke briefly. Milo saw the mayor smile. She shrugged. Then, the mayor returned. Problem solved! the mayor called out. Great news! When will the bridge be done? Milo asked hopefully. Completed? No. Too many problems. We're throwing in the towel! Mayor McQuitter replied.

Name: _____

Date: _____

Handout 25A: Focusing Question Task 3 Checklist

Directions: Use this checklist to help you assess and revise your writing. Mark + for "yes" and Δ for "not yet." You may ask someone (adult or peer) to evaluate your writing as well.

Focusing Question Task 3 "Exploded Moment" Writing Checklist	Self +/ Δ	Peer +/ Δ	Teacher +/ Δ
Reading Comprehension			
• I create an "exploded moment" that focuses on an interaction between Milo and my character from Focusing Question Task 2.			
• I introduce a conflict between Milo and my character related to their ideas about school and learning.			
• My conflict, resolution, and descriptions of my setting and my character involve a play on the meaning of abandon and my character's name.			
• I use dialogue to move the story forward and to reveal an important learning Milo has.			
Structure			
• In my lead, I establish: 　o characters, including Milo and my character; 　o the setting, Abandon Elementary School; 　o a situation, or scene, in which Milo meets my character.			
• My story's action centers mainly on an interaction between Milo and my character, including a conflict between the characters' ideas about school and learning.			
• I provide an ending that follows logically from the action and reveals new learning or understanding that Milo gains as a result of this interaction.			
• I organize my events in a natural order.			
• I use transitions to tie details and events together.			

Name: _____

Date: _____

Development			
• I use dialogue between Milo and my character to develop the conflict, show the characters' responses to each other's ideas, and move the story forward.			
• I alternate between dialogue and narration to show what characters are doing and thinking in addition to what they are saying.			
• I use concrete and sensory details to describe my setting and characters and reinforce wordplay with the meaning of abandon and my character's name.			
Style			
• My writing style is appropriate for the audience.			
• I choose precise words—including vivid verbs and concrete, sensory details—to add detail to my writing and make my character come alive for readers.			
Conventions			
• I format dialogue by beginning a new paragraph each time a different person speaks.			
• I punctuate dialogue by placing quotation marks around a speaker's exact words.			
• I add commas to separate speaker tags (e.g., she said, he asked) from the direct quotation.			
• I include at least one interjection in my dialogue and place a comma after it.			
• I include at least one tag question in dialogue and place a comma before it.			
• I include at least one noun of direct address in dialogue and set it off from the rest of the sentence with a comma or commas.			
Writing Process			
• I revise my exploded moment to: 　o clarify the conflict between my characters; and 　o add narration to my dialogue exchange to help my readers visualize what my characters are doing and thinking.			
Total number of +'s:			

Handout 26A: Fluency Homework

Directions:
1. Day 1: Read the text carefully and annotate to help you read fluently.
2. Each day:
    a. Practice reading the text three to five times.
    b. Evaluate your progress by placing a ✓+, ✓, or ✓- in each unshaded box.
    c. Ask someone (adult or peer) to listen and evaluate you as well.
3. Last day: Respond to the self-reflection questions.

"I hope you found what you were looking for."

"I'm afraid not," admitted Milo. And then he added in a very discouraged tone, "Everything in Digitopolis is much too difficult for me."

The Mathemagician nodded knowingly and stroked his chin several times. "You'll find," he remarked gently, "that the only thing you can do easily is be wrong, and that's hardly worth the effort."

Milo tried very hard to understand all the things he'd been told, and all the things he'd seen, and, as he spoke, one curious thing still bothered him. "Why is it," he said quietly, "that quite often even the things which are correct just don't seem to be right?"

A look of deep melancholy crossed the Mathemagician's face and his eyes grew moist with sadness. Everything was silent, and it was several minutes before he was able to reply at all.

"How very true," he sobbed, supporting himself on the staff. "It has been that way since Rhyme and Reason were banished."

Juster, Norton. *The Phantom Tollbooth*. New York: Random House, 1961. Print.

Name: _____

Date: _____

Student Performance Checklist:	Day 1		Day 2		Day 3	
	You	Listener*	You	Listener*	You	Listener*
Accurately read the passage 3–5 times.						
Read with appropriate phrasing and pausing.						
Read with appropriate expression.						
Read articulately at a good pace, and an audible volume.						

*Adult or peer

Self-reflection: What choices did you make when deciding how to read this passage, and why? What would you like to improve on or try differently next time? (*Thoughtfully answer these questions on this paper.*)

G5 > M2 > Handout 27A • WIT & WISDOM™

Name: _____

Date: _____

Handout 27A: Demons of Ignorance

Directions: Complete the following chart to further your understanding of Milo's transformation in *The Phantom Tollbooth*.

Demon's Name and Its Meaning:

Description of Demon	Challenge to Milo	Milo's Use of Gift	Conquering Ignorance
Appearance – What does this demon look like?	How does this demon present a challenge or obstacle to Milo's quest? In other words, how does this demon try to keep Milo in "ignorance"?	How does Milo use one of his gifts to overcome this challenge and help him conquer "ignorance"?	**Change** – Based on Milo's actions and how he uses a gift to conquer this demon, what can you infer about how he has changed?
Wordplay – How is this demon's name an example of wordplay? In other words, how do his behaviors and traits reflect his name?			**Lesson** – What lesson could Milo learn about conquering ignorance by using this gift?

Handout 28A: Demons of Ignorance Homework

Directions: Complete the following chart to further your understanding of Milo's transformation in *The Phantom Tollbooth*.

Demon's Name and Its Meaning:	**Senses Taker**
	senses (n.): any of five ways to experience your environment; the senses are touch, smell, taste, sight, and hearing
	census (n.): an official count of the people who live in a country or other area. A census is also used to collect information about these people, such as their job, age, or sex.

Description of Demon	Challenge to Milo	Milo's Use of Gift	Conquering Ignorance
Appearance – What does this demon look like?	**Challenge to Milo** – How does this demon present a challenge or obstacle to Milo's quest? In other words, how does this demon try to keep Milo in "ignorance"?	**Milo's Use of Gift** – How does Milo use one of his gifts to overcome this challenge and help him conquer "ignorance"?	**Change** – Based on Milo's actions and how he uses a gift to conquer this demon, what can you infer about how he has changed?
Wordplay – How is this demon's name an example of wordplay? In other words, how do his behaviors and traits reflect his name?			**Lesson** – What lesson could Milo learn about conquering ignorance by using this gift?

Handout 29A: Rhyme and Reason's Advice

Directions: Complete the following chart to further your understanding of how the advice Milo receives from the princesses can help him resolve internal conflicts.

Name: _____

Date: _____

Milo's Internal Conflicts	Advice from Rhyme and Reason	Resolving a Conflict *How could Rhyme and Reason's advice help Milo resolve his internal conflicts?*
	"You must never feel badly about making mistakes…as long as you take the trouble to learn from them" (233).	Rhyme and Reason's advice could help Milo resolve his conflict by…
	"…you often learn more by being wrong for the right reasons than you do by being right for the wrong ones" (233).	Rhyme and Reason's advice could help Milo resolve his conflict by…

Name: _____

Date: _____

Rhyme and Reason's advice could help Milo resolve his conflict by…

"…it's not just learning things that's important. It's learning what to do with what you learn and learning why you learn things at all that matters" (233).

"You may not see it now…but whatever we learn has a purpose and whatever we do affects everything and everyone else, if even in the tiniest way…it's much the same with knowledge, for whenever you learn something new, the whole world becomes that much richer" (233–34).

"…many places you would like to see are just off the map and many things you want to know are just out of sight…But someday you'll reach them all, for what you learn today, for no reason at all, will help you discover all the wonderful secrets of tomorrow" (234).

Handout 29B: Fluency Homework

Directions:
1. Day 1: Read the text carefully and annotate to help you read fluently.
2. Each day:
    a. Practice reading the text three to five times.
    b. Evaluate your progress by placing a ✓+, ✓, or ✓- in each unshaded box.
    c. Ask someone (adult or peer) to listen and evaluate you as well.
3. Last day: Respond to the self-reflection questions.

"…it's not just learning things that's important. It's learning what to do with what you learn and learning why you learn things at all that matters."

"That's just what I mean," explained Milo as Tock and the exhausted bug drifted quietly off to sleep. "Many of the things I'm supposed to know seem so useless that I can't see the purpose in learning them at all."

"You may not see it now," said the Princess of Pure Reason, looking knowingly at Milo's puzzled face, "but whatever we learn has a purpose and whatever we do affects everything else, if even in the tiniest way. Why, when a housefly flaps his wings, a breeze goes round the world; when a speck of dust falls to the ground, the entire planet weighs a little more; and when you stamp your foot, the earth moves slightly off its course. Whenever you laugh, gladness spreads like the ripples in a pond; and whenever you're sad, no one anywhere can be really happy. And it's much the same thing with knowledge, for whenever you learn something new, the whole world becomes that much richer."

Juster, Norton. *The Phantom Tollbooth*. New York: Random House, 1961. Print.

Name: _____

Date: _____

Student Performance Checklist:	Day 1		Day 2		Day 3	
	You	Listener*	You	Listener*	You	Listener*
Accurately read the passage 3-5 times.						
Read with appropriate phrasing and pausing.						
Read with appropriate expression.						
Read articulately at a good pace, and an audible volume.						

*Adult or peer

Self-reflection: What choices did you make when deciding how to read this passage, and why? What would you like to improve on or try differently next time? (*Thoughtfully answer these questions on this paper.*)

Name:

Date:

Handout 32A: Theme Paragraph Planner

Directions: Use this planner to help you organize your ideas for your explanatory "theme" paragraph. Remember, your goal is to help your reader To SEE Clearly.

Topic Statement **(To S)**	*For the first part of your topic statement, state one overarching theme of The Phantom Tollbooth. (Your theme statement should relate to the changes you've seen in Milo over the course of the book.)* *For the second part of your topic statement, describe one important way that Milo has transformed or changed to support your theme statement.*
Evidence and Elaboration **(E)** **(E)**	*Cite evidence from the story of Milo's transformation to support your theme statement, and <u>elaborate</u> on how the <u>evidence</u> connects to this theme.* • <u>Evidence</u> of what Milo was like at the beginning of the story, related to your theme: • <u>Elaborate</u> on what this evidence reveals about Milo and how it connects to the theme:

Name: _____

Date: _____

Evidence and Elaboration (E) (E)	*Cite evidence from the story of Milo's transformation to support your theme statement, and elaborate on how the evidence connects to this theme.* • <u>Evidence</u> of what Milo was like at the beginning of the story, related to your theme: • <u>Elaborate</u> on what this evidence reveals about Milo and how it connects to the theme:
Concluding statement (C)	*Reinforce your essential idea, or the theme you've identified, and reflect on how Juster develops it over the course of the story.*

Handout 33A: *Reading at a Table*

Directions: Read the following museum label for Pablo Picasso's *Reading at a Table*. Be ready to share what types of information should be included in a museum label.

Pablo Picasso
Reading at a Table
1934
Oil on canvas

This painting portrays a woman sitting at a table wearing a crown of greenery, reading a book peacefully. She appears in a comfortable home with a large plant, a lamp, and a framed image on the wall. Picasso chose light, cheerful colors to depict her face and body contrasted against a dark, cozy interior. The soft curving lines define the woman's body as well as other objects in the room. Picasso's use of soft colors and lines communicates his affection for his young girlfriend.

Name: _____

Date: _____

Handout 33B: Museum Label for Magritte

Directions: Use the following planner to write a museum label for your assigned painting.

Magritte
Title (Write a title for the painting):   1938   Oil on canvas
What is the essential meaning of the painting?

G5 > M2 > Handout 33C • WIT & WISDOM™

Name:

Date:

Handout 33C: Museum Label for Dalí

Directions: Use the following planner to write a museum label for your assigned painting.

Dalí
Title (Write a title for the painting):   1931   Oil on Canvas
What is the essential meaning of the painting?

Name: _____

Date: _____

Handout 33D: Focusing Question Task 4 Checklist

Directions: Use the following checklist to ensure you have met the expectations for Focusing Question Task 4.

Explanatory Paragraph Writing Checklist	Self +/ Δ	Peer +/ Δ	Teacher +/ Δ
Reading Comprehension			
• I explain one central theme from the novel *The Phantom Tollbooth*.			
• I explain how Milo's transformation in the story supports this theme.			
• I quote accurately from the text as needed to provide evidence to support my ideas.			
Structure			
• I respond to all parts of the prompt.			
• I focus on my topic throughout the paragraph.			

• I provide a two-part topic statement that includes:
   o A theme statement about a central theme in *The Phantom Tollbooth*.
   o A statement describing an important change in Milo that supports this theme.			

• I organize my ideas in the body of my paragraph.			
• My concluding statement reinforces the theme and reflects on how Norton Juster develops it over the course of the story.			
Development			
• I provide relevant evidence from the story to support the theme, including one or two quotations showing what Milo was like at the beginning of the story and how he changes.			
• I elaborate on my evidence to explain how it connects to and/or supports the theme.			

Name: _____

Date: _____

Style			
• I include introductory elements in my sentences to add variety to sentences or provide background information.			
Conventions			
• I use commas to correctly punctuate introductory elements.			
• I place quotation marks around quoted text and include the page number in parentheses after the ending quotation marks and before the period.			
• I use correct spelling, punctuation, and capitalization.			
Total number of +'s:			

Name: _____

Date: _____

Handout 34A: Demon Analysis

Directions: Complete the following chart by using what you know about your group's demon from the Mountains of Ignorance.

Demon: _____

1. What faulty, confusing, or wrong belief does this demon have, related to his name? This demon believes that…   2. Give your demon a nickname based on his faulty thinking.
3. How could your demon's faulty, or wrong, beliefs (related to his name) create problems for him? In other words, how could your demon's way of thinking cause him to have a problem? Brainstorm two problems here. One problem this demon could face is…   A second problem this demon could face is…

Name: _____

Date: _____

4. What has Milo learned in the Lands Beyond that could help this character change his faulty, or wrong, beliefs? In other words, what wisdom could Milo share, related to the book's themes, to help this demon with his problem? How did Milo learn this lesson?

The wisdom Milo could share is…

Milo learned this lesson by…

Name: _____

Date: _____

Handout 35A: Dialogue Planner for End-of-Module Task

Directions: Think about the transformation that Milo has undergone in the story and how it relates to overarching themes in the book. What wisdom could Milo give your demon to help him solve his problem? Then, think about each character's beliefs about the idea that has caused a problem for the demon. Draft lines of dialogue and narration, in which you clearly convey the problem, Milo's wisdom, and what the demon learns from him.

1. The Problem My demon's big problem is…	**2. The Lesson** Milo could help my demon by teaching him a lesson or sharing wisdom about…
3. Milo's Ideas In this conversation, Milo thinks…	**4. My Demon's Ideas** In this same conversation, my demon thinks…

Wordplay Ideas/Phrases
How can you play with the meanings of your demon's name in their conversation?

G5 > M2 > Handout 35A • WIT & WISDOM™

Name: _____

Date: _____

Milo

My Demon: _____

G5 > M2 > Handout 35A • WIT & WISDOM™

Name:

Date:

Name:

Date:

Name: _____

Date: _____

Handout 36A: End-of-Module Task Checklist

Directions: Use the checklist below to revise your draft exploded moment scene.

Grades 4–5 Narrative Writing Checklist	Self +/ △	Peer +/ △	Teacher +/ △
Focus on Task and Text			
• I understand the prompt.			
• I respond to all parts of the prompt.			
• I create an "exploded moment" that focuses on the interaction between Milo and a demon from *The Phantom Tollbooth*.			
• I introduce a conflict that my demon faces, related to his name and the idea he represents.			
• I use dialogue to show what characters are like, develop the conflict and resolution, and show an important "learning" by the demon.			
• My description of my demon reflects his name and continues the wordplay of his name.			
Structure			
• I establish characters, setting, and a situation at the beginning of my narrative.			
• My story's action centers mainly on the interaction between Milo and my demon.			
• I organize my events in a natural order.			
• My conclusion follows from the narrated events, sticks with readers, and conveys a central theme of *The Phantom Tollbooth*.			
• I use transitions to clearly sequence events.			

Name: _____

Date: _____

Development and Support			
• I use dialogue between Milo and my demon to develop the conflict and action, show the characters' responses to one another, and convey theme.			
• I alternate between dialogue and narration to show what characters are doing and thinking in addition to what they are saying.			
• I use description and sensory details to develop characters and setting and "show" not "tell."			
Style			
• I use a variety of sentence patterns (simple, compound, complex).			
• I added variety to at least two sentences by adding an introductory element.			
• My writing style is appropriate for the audience.			
• I choose precise words—including vivid verbs; concrete, or specific, details; and prepositional phrases—to add detail to my writing and "show-not-tell."			
Conventions			
• I use correct spelling, capitalization, and punctuation.			
• I correctly punctuate dialogue with quotation marks, commas, end marks, and indented lines for each new speaker.			
• I use commas to set off interjections, tag questions, nouns of direct address, and introductory elements from the rest of the sentence.			
Writing process			
• I revise my writing to include stronger descriptive narration to "show-not-tell."			
Total number of +'s:			

Volume of Reading Reflection Questions

Word Play, Grade 5, Module 2

Student Name: _____

Text: _____

Author: _____

Topic: _____

Genre/Type of Book: _____

Share your knowledge about the wordplay culture by answering the questions below.

Informational Text

1. Wonder: How might this text teach you about wordplay? Provide three details that support your response.

2. Organize: Summarize the main ideas and key details of the text, including key details about wordplay.

3. Reveal: How does the author make the information about language interesting? Describe at least two techniques the author uses.

4. Distill: How does this text support or challenge what you already knew about how language can be used to entertain and inform? Provide at least three examples.

5. Know: How did this text build your knowledge? Explain an important idea about language, supporting the idea with details from this text and at least one other text.

6. Vocabulary: What are three words you will use in a new way because of this text? Use each of these words in a creative sentence.

Literary Text:

1. Wonder: Why did you choose this book? How do you think the story might connect to language?

2. Organize: Write a short summary of the story, including the major character(s), setting, problem, and resolution.

3. Reveal: How does language impact the story? Provide examples from the text.

4. Distill: What is a theme of this story? Provide evidence from the text to support your response.

5. Know: How does the language in this story compare and contrast with another story?

6. Vocabulary: What are three words from the text that the main character would identify as important to them? Write a sentence with each of these words from the character's perspective.

WIT & WISDOM PARENT TIP SHEET

WHAT IS MY FIFTH-GRADE STUDENT LEARNING IN MODULE 2?

Wit & Wisdom is our English curriculum. It builds knowledge of key topics in history, science, and literature through the study of excellent texts. By reading and responding to stories and nonfiction texts, we will build knowledge of the following topics:

Module 1: Cultures in Conflict

Module 2: Word Play

Module 3: A War Between Us

Module 4: Breaking Barriers

In this second module, *Word Play*, we will study the way we use words to define and organize our world. We will read playful stories to investigate wordplay and answer the question, *How and why do writers play with words?*

OUR CLASS WILL READ THIS TEXT

Novel

- *The Phantom Tollbooth*, Norton Juster

OUR CLASS WILL EXAMINE THESE PAINTINGS:

- *The Persistence of Memory*, Salvador Dalí
- *Time Transfixed*, René Magritte

OUR CLASS WILL WATCH THIS VIDEO:

- "Who's on First?" Bud Abbott and Lou Costello

OUR CLASS WILL ASK THESE QUESTIONS:

- How can wordplay create confusion and humor?
- How can writers use wordplay to develop a story's settings and characters?
- How can writers use wordplay to develop a story's plot?
- How is *The Phantom Tollbooth* a story of transformation?

QUESTIONS TO ASK AT HOME:

As your fifth-grade student reads, ask:

- What's happening?
- What does a closer look at words and illustrations reveal about this text's deeper meaning?

BOOKS TO READ AT HOME:

- *The Right Word: Roget and His Thesaurus*, Jen Bryant and Melissa Sweet
- *A River of Words: The Story of William Carlos Williams*, Jen Bryant and Melissa Sweet
- *Noah Webster: Weaver of Words*, Pegi Deitz Shea
- *The Dreamer*, Pam Muñoz Ryan and Peter Sís
- *Rain Reign*, Ann M. Martin
- *Lemonade and Other Poems Squeezed from a Single Word*, Bob Raczka
- *C B D!*, William Steig

IDEAS FOR TALKING ABOUT LANGUAGE:

Playing with words together is a lot of fun. Try word games like this one at home:

Hink Pink: One person thinks of two rhyming words, like "fat cat" or "lead bed." That person shares a clue so his or her partner can guess the rhyming words, such as "a large feline" (fat cat) or "a heavy sleeping place" (lead bed).

A few to get you started:

- Soaked animal in the house (wet pet)
- Seafood dreams (fish wish)
- Playground at night (dark park)

CREDITS

Great Minds® has made every effort to obtain permission for the reprinting of all copyrighted material. If any owner of copyrighted material is not acknowledged herein, please contact Great Minds® for proper acknowledgment in all future editions and reprints of this module.

- All material from the *Common Core State Standards for English Language Arts & Literacy in History/Social Studies, Science, and Technical Subjects* © Copyright 2010 National Governors Association Center for Best Practices and Council of Chief State School Officers. All rights reserved.
- All images are used under license from Shutterstock.com unless otherwise noted.
- For updated credit information, please visit http://witeng.link/credits.

ACKNOWLEDGMENTS

Great Minds® Staff

The following writers, editors, reviewers, and support staff contributed to the development of this curriculum.

Ann Brigham, Lauren Chapalee, Sara Clarke, Emily Climer, Lorraine Griffith, Emily Gula, Sarah Henchey, Trish Huerster, Stephanie Kane-Mainier, Lior Klirs, Liz Manolis, Andrea Minich, Lynne Munson, Marya Myers, Rachel Rooney, Aaron Schifrin, Danielle Shylit, Rachel Stack, Sarah Turnage, Michelle Warner, Amy Wierzbicki, Margaret Wilson, and Sarah Woodard.

Colleagues and Contributors

We are grateful for the many educators, writers, and subject-matter experts who made this program possible.

David Abel, Robin Agurkis, Elizabeth Bailey, Julianne Barto, Amy Benjamin, Andrew Biemiller, Charlotte Boucher, Sheila Byrd-Carmichael, Eric Carey, Jessica Carloni, Janine Cody, Rebecca Cohen, Elaine Collins, Tequila Cornelious, Beverly Davis, Matt Davis, Thomas Easterling, Jeanette Edelstein, Kristy Ellis, Moira Clarkin Evans, Charles Fischer, Marty Gephart, Kath Gibbs, Natalie Goldstein, Christina Gonzalez, Mamie Goodson, Nora Graham, Lindsay Griffith, Brenna Haffner, Joanna Hawkins, Elizabeth Haydel, Steve Hettleman, Cara Hoppe, Ashley Hymel, Carol Jago, Jennifer Johnson, Mason Judy, Gail Kearns, Shelly Knupp, Sarah Kushner, Shannon Last, Suzanne Lauchaire, Diana Leddy, David Liben, Farren Liben, Jennifer Marin, Susannah Maynard, Cathy McGath, Emily McKean, Jane Miller, Rebecca Moore, Cathy Newton, Turi Nilsson, Julie Norris, Galemarie Ola, Michelle Palmieri, Meredith Phillips, Shilpa Raman, Tonya Romayne, Emmet Rosenfeld, Jennifer Ruppel, Mike Russoniello, Deborah Samley, Casey Schultz, Renee Simpson, Rebecca Sklepovich, Amelia Swabb, Kim Taylor, Vicki Taylor, Melissa Thomson, Lindsay Tomlinson, Melissa Vail, Keenan Walsh, Julia Wasson, Lynn Welch, Yvonne Guerrero Welch, Emily Whyte, Lynn Woods, and Rachel Zindler.

Early Adopters

The following early adopters provided invaluable insight and guidance for Wit & Wisdom:

- Bourbonnais School District 53 • Bourbonnais, IL
- Coney Island Prep Middle School • Brooklyn, NY
- Gate City Charter School for the Arts • Merrimack, NH
- Hebrew Academy for Special Children • Brooklyn, NY
- Paris Independent Schools • Paris, KY
- Saydel Community School District • Saydel, IA
- Strive Collegiate Academy • Nashville, TN
- Valiente College Preparatory Charter School • South Gate, CA
- Voyageur Academy • Detroit, MI

Design Direction provided by Alton Creative, Inc.
Project management support, production design and copyediting services provided by ScribeConcepts.com
Copyediting services provided by Fine Lines Editing
Product management support provided by Sandhill Consulting